THE

rebuilt

FIELD GUIDE

"In *Rebuilt* many of us awakened to a new reality—the greatest threat to the Church's core mission is relying on the status quo. For all who responded, 'Yes, but now what?' welcome to White and Corcoran's field guide! This is the most practical and effective tool I've seen to help parish leaders plot a course from holy discontent to making church matter."

Claire Henning
Executive Director
Parish Catalyst

"*The Rebuilt Field Guide* provides a wonderfully simple, straightforward, step-by-step process for any pastor and staff looking to begin the process of rebuilding their parish so that they can zero in on the mission of making disciples."

Rev. Michael Jones
Pastor
St. Pius X Catholic Church, Bowie, Maryland

"This is exactly what we needed to begin implementing culture change in our parish. White and Corcoran share how to stick to your vision while tackling the challenges you'll face, and it is truly inspiring. I can't wait to share this with the rest of our leadership and staff!"

David Landa
Director of Pastoral Life
St. Philip the Apostle Parish, Pasadena, California

"The church staff meeting has just been taken to a new level! This resource will help any parish team to grow together dynamically—and their church will never be the same again!"

Rev. Michael A. Saporito
Pastor
Parish Community of St. Helen, Westfield, New Jersey

"Never in my twenty-three years of ministry have I found more effective tools than those given in *Rebuilt* and now in *The Rebuilt Field Guide*. My parishioners are actually talking about the effect the parish is having in their lives."

Rev. Brian Mason
Pastor
St. Mary's Parish, Hales Corners, Wisconsin

"This is mandatory reading for anyone taking the call to the New Evangelization seriously!"

Katie Skerpon
Small-Group Coordinator
St. Pius X Catholic Church, Bowie, Maryland

THE
rebuilt
FIELD GUIDE

Ten Steps for

Getting Started

Michael White and Tom Corcoran

Ave Maria Press AVE Notre Dame, Indiana

Founded in 1865, Ave Maria Press is a ministry of the United States Province of Holy Cross.

www.avemariapress.com

Paperback: ISBN-13 978-1-59471-701-7

E-book: ISBN-13 978-1-59471-702-4

Cover and text design by Katherine J. Ross.

Printed and bound in the United States of America.

Library of Congress Cataloging-in-Publication Data

Names: White, Michael, 1958- author. | Corcoran, Tom, author. | White, Michael, 1958- author. Rebuilt.
Title: The rebuilt field guide : ten steps for getting started / Michael White and Tom Corcoran.
Description: Notre Dame, Indiana : Ave Maria Press, 2016. | Includes bibliographical references.
Identifiers: LCCN 2016019602 (print) | LCCN 2016031713 (ebook) | ISBN 9781594717017 | ISBN 159471701X | ISBN 9781594717024 () | ISBN 1594717028 ()
Subjects: LCSH: Church renewal--Catholic Church.
Classification: LCC BX1746 .W4954 2016 (print) | LCC BX1746 (ebook) | DDC 253--dc23
LC record available at https://lccn.loc.gov/2016019602

CONTENTS

BEFORE YOU BEGIN

The officers went through the camp
and issued these commands to the people:
"When you see the ark of the covenant . . . follow it,
that you may know the way." . . .
Joshua also said to the people, "Sanctify yourselves,
for tomorrow the Lord will perform wonders among
you."

JOSHUA 3:2–5

This is a book about the local community church
that Catholics call their parish. We're two guys who
have been working in a parish for a few years. That's
probably our essential qualification for writing this
book. Actually, it's our only qualification, and to tell
you the truth, for a long time we weren't even any
good at it.

REBUILT, XV

Rebuilt tells the story of what happened to us, what we learned, and what we now know about growing a healthy parish. It is all about the twin exercises of discipleship and evangelization, or what we have come to call awakening the faithful, while also, and at the same time, reaching the lost—oh, and in the process, making church matter.

The formation, composition, and publication of the book were a challenging, surprising, and ultimately thrilling experience. All of it was unlikely and therefore unexpected. It was also life changing.

One of the things that changed markedly about our lives was the sudden interest we attracted and the new demands on our time. It quickly became commonplace for visitors from other parishes to show up at our church any time of the week and throughout the weekend. We actually started regularly assigning staff to be on visitor duty. There were plenty of calls and cards, letters, and e-mail too. Invitations to speak throughout the country and even further afield began arriving.

Basically, all the interest came down to the same thing: "Tell us how to do it; tell us how to grow a healthy parish." And that is something we very much wanted to do. The only problem was, despite our best intentions, we simply could not help everyone who reached out to us (and run our own parish at the same time).

In our second book, *Tools for Rebuilding*, we shared many practical tools to getting started in parish renewal when it comes to discipleship and evangelization. More recently, it occurred to us that a guide to rebuilding in the deep weeds of parish life might also be helpful. That's where this book started taking shape.

In it, you will find very little that comes as news, perhaps nothing at all that you didn't already know. We do not pretend to suggest there are many original insights here. In fact, it's all rather simple and straightforward. We just want to share with you what works when it comes to evangelization and discipleship in our parish in Timonium, Maryland.

We'll tell you exactly how we did and continue to do things here. Then, you apply or adapt what you think might work in your setting and, in the process, learn more about what actually does work for you. It matters not at all what kind of parish you have: big or small, urban or rural, affluent or struggling. To undertake these exercises, you don't need any particular resources, additional staff, or budget, and you won't have to hire a consultant. You really only need one thing: *a team.*

Rebuilding your parish is not a solitary effort. Ideally, it is a team exercise led by the pastor or parish pastoral leader. It also includes at least a few people who are willing to think creatively while speaking honestly about the problems and opportunities that really exist. The team must understand that there are no quick fixes or silver bullets. Neither are there any grand strategies waiting to be discovered.

The ten steps we suggest here are not ten *weeks,* nor are they ten *meetings.* They are ten starting points that introduce your team to exercises for rebuilding.

Taken together, these exercises are a disciplined march in a single direction. The team must have a commitment to a sustained, long-term effort in parish renewal and rebuilding.

Most of all, the team must have trust in one another, and be willing to work collaboratively and with mutual respect. Listening and learning will be essential for such trust, and humor and humility will help a lot too.

That's the complicated part. Once you've got a team in place, the rest is simple. It's not *easy.* Like any exercise regime, the one suggested here will require a lot of hard work and heavy lifting, and that won't be easy. But it is simple.

Each section or chapter of this field guide will walk you and your team through a series of exercises. Each begins in prayer and includes storytelling, to help the team understand the history and the context of what is happening. And the exercises end in some specific resolution, or steps to take toward introducing change and moving forward.

Finally, we offer what we're calling the "rally cry," a term we're borrowing from our friend Patrick Lencioni. The rally cry is a phrase that brings your team together to support a shared idea or undertake a common cause. It best represents what your team is trying to accomplish. The rally cry is the main thing, perhaps the *one* thing, that must be done now.

It's a cry to do things differently, creating a kind of discontent that is meant to motivate. Because the rally cry springs from our Christ-given mission to make disciples, that discontent is, in a sense, sacred. We'll be calling it a "holy discontent," a phrase we also borrowed, in this case from Pastor Bill Hybels.

Parish life is currently changing quickly. So, like life for the people of Israel in the Exodus, all of us in parish ministry find ourselves in a place we've never been before. And, like Joshua, effective parish leaders will form the resolve to move forward in strategic and bold ways. We hope what follows helps.

HOW TO USE THIS GUIDE

Tom: If you are like Father Michael, you'll obsess over this guide and each of its "how tos."

Father Michael: And if you're like Tom, you'll skip over the "how tos" and just dive right in.

Don't do either. In view of the following, take time to consider how you will proceed and then do so confidently. Each chapter of this guide is intended to form an exercise or a series of exercises for your team. Depending on your circumstances, any particular exercise might require multiple sessions to work through. (It may even take months.) Don't rush these exercises; take the time you need. Here are some additional steps that will make this guide more useful and your work more successful.

Assemble the Team

The pastor or pastoral leader needs to put in plenty of thought and prayer on the front end about who joins the team. Just because someone is on staff or they simply want to be a part of the team doesn't mean they qualify. Just because someone agrees with the pastor doesn't mean they qualify either. More useful qualities include a lively faith, a commitment to the parish, demonstrated willingness to serve, emotional health, and an ability to think creatively. Together the team should present a balanced cross-section of your parish, mindful of ethnic diversity.

Though not everyone on the team needs a long-term relationship with the parish, at least one member should have solid institutional memory. On the other hand, a newcomer, who brings fresh perspective, would be especially valuable too. The team should not be less than five or more than eight, a size intended to accommodate robust discussion.

Set the Ground Rules

Your team is not going to be very effective if they just show up for meetings and start shooting from the hip with a lot of preconceived notions and intransigent opinions. These exercises will not be fruitful if individual members are only concerned with what they think, what they like, and what they want. The team is not even a team, and will go nowhere, if people are only there to advance their own agendas or defend their silo ministries.

Before the very first session, you will want to set rules of engagement for your time together. You also might need to review these rules before each subsequent session. A short list should include confidentiality, trust, a commitment to speaking the truth in love, and active listening. Invite team members to study Patrick Lencioni's excellent resource *Death By Meeting*.

Prepare the Exercises

These exercises require preparation, much like any good workout requires a warmup. Most chapters come with a reading assignment from *Rebuilt* that should be read before the exercises begin. Also read the "Consider" sections in each chapter and come with prepared notes to address the sections marked "Tell Your Story." The best way to tell your story is to *prepare* your story.

You will need to decide who will facilitate meetings. By the way, it doesn't have to be and maybe shouldn't be the pastor. Perhaps, someone with leadership experience or listening skills can perform this task best. This can free other team members to focus exclusively on the work at hand rather than everyone trying to work out the process details as you move forward. Or you may decide to take turns leading entire meetings or various parts of meetings. For example, one person might lead prayer, another guides the storytelling, and a third directs brainstorming and setting priorities.

Additionally you will need to decide as a group, or as individuals leading particular activities, just how exercises such as brainstorming, prioritizing, planning next steps, and reaching resolutions will be structured. These don't need to be complicated processes, but someone should come up with a plan for how to prioritize a list of desired changes. We simply prompt you to "prioritize," assuming you will come up with the best method for your own group. Start by deciding if an exercise should be done first by individuals and then as a group or by simply launching into the exercise as a group activity.

Facilitators will also need to decide simple things such as if you will need a flip chart, whiteboard, or PowerPoint and what needs to be made ready ahead of time. Snacks and drinks help; a comfortable well-lit setting is essential. Without careful planning for the little things (think who, what, where, when, and how), the bigger tasks of rebuilding will be frustrated.

Think and Pray

Team members should be talking to parishioners and others in the community about the exercise topics. You will do well to challenge yourselves to think about the parish in new ways, perhaps to think bigger.

The team must be lifting up each exercise in prayer, and the parish should be praying for the team and the exercises as well. An especially helpful approach is to recruit a prayer team to pray while you are meeting. Or consider offering holy hours for the whole parish that coincide with meeting times. That way everyone is invited—even encouraged—to play a crucial part in the rebuilding.

1

BE HONEST ABOUT
THE REAL PROBLEMS

You see the trouble we are in:
how Jerusalem lies in ruins
and its gates have been gutted by fire.
Come, let us rebuild.

NEHEMIAH 2:17

We seek to thoughtfully address all of you who are concerned that things in many parishes do not seem to be going well these days. A single, simple fact establishes the problem: One in three Catholics has walked away from the Church, making "former Catholic" the third largest religious designation in the country.

REBUILT, XVI

PREPARE BY READING
Rebuilt: introduction and chapter 1

Consider

The point of *The Rebuilt Field Guide* is to help you create and sustain change that will enable your team to grow a healthy (or healthier) parish. Change happens when you develop both an intellectual understanding of what needs to change as well as a heartfelt desire to actually do it. And then you need a plan to make it happen. That's the story of Nehemiah, who learns about the distressed condition of Jerusalem, comes to grieve this situation, and determines to rebuild.

This first exercise should help you develop the intellectual understanding of what the situation really is in your parish. But of equal importance is your team's willingness to consider why the status quo or business as usual is no longer acceptable to you.

If this is an honest exercise, it will be a painful one. Try to establish a professional tone, keep the discussion above personalities and recriminations. Strive to maintain a frank dialogue about the facts. But even if you accomplish these things—if it's an honest process—it is going to be painful. And that's okay. As is often said in recovery, "When the pain of where you are is greater than where you need to be, then you'll move." If you're reading this book, the pain of where you are is probably greater than the pain of what you need to do.

Change in our parish began when we came to recognize the pain we were experiencing. We were working very hard, but nothing was ever any different *after* than *before* all our efforts. We were used up and burned out despite our very best efforts. Through this step, you will reflect on your parish's history and identify the problems that you need to address.

Pray

Pray together. Begin in silent prayer; then add spontaneous prayers of thanksgiving and petition. Include intercessory prayer for current problems and needs, as well as prayer of thanksgiving for those who have helped make the story of the parish happen. Then pray:

> Heavenly Father,
> you gave your servant Nehemiah a heart to serve you
> as he led the great project of rebuilding the walls of Jerusalem.
> Lead our own rebuilding effort
> and give us the heart to serve you wisely and generously
> here in our parish, in our generation.
> We pray through Christ, our Lord.
> Amen.

Tell Your Story

Members, in turn, should share with the rest of the team a little bit about their background, family life, professional pursuits. Invite everyone to tell the story of how they came to the parish and what they've been involved in since then.

Rebuilt describes some of the history of Church of the Nativity. Knowing your community's story can be very helpful when it comes to uniting your team and making progress toward your goal (not to mention avoiding past mistakes). Take a moment to recount anecdotal stories from the life of your parish. If it seems helpful, bring in senior members of the congregation who have longer institutional memories and ask them to share stories too. Try to work your various memories into a more cohesive narrative, identifying themes that might emerge. Have one team member write these themes on a flip chart or whiteboard so you are all looking at the same words.

Does the history of the parish, especially its successes and achievements, suggest anything when it comes to what God wants to do in the future of the parish? Brainstorm ideas, again posting them where everyone can see.

Read Aloud

The following is excerpted and modified from Rebuilt, *pages 5–7. We suggest breaking the reading into parts and having more than one reader. Check the boxes corresponding to your experience.*

Our own lack of excitement and vision about being at the parish perfectly matched the attitude we found here. What we discovered at Nativity in the late '90s was a languid community aging in place. To better assess the situation in our first year, we engaged Georgetown University's Center for Applied Research in the Apostolate to survey our congregation. When asked what attracted them to this church, 96 percent of parishioners identified "convenient parking" as the number one reason they were here. Here are a few others things we discovered (as you read through this list, check off every one that describes your parish right now):

- ☐ Kids hated our religious education program, and it was nearly impossible to find all the volunteer teachers we needed; nobody wanted to do it.
- ☐ There was no youth ministry; teenagers and young adults were no-shows at the church.
- ☐ The music wasn't bad: It was painfully, ear-achingly, "please, please, please, for the love of God stop!" bad.
- ☐ A line-up of rotating priest-celebrants guaranteed an uneven quality of preaching and, sometimes, conflicting messages.

☐ The experience of weekend Masses was moribund and depressing. We wouldn't have attended this church if we didn't work here.

☐ The congregation's level of giving wasn't paying the bills (and we had a bare-bones budget to say the least). Some recent years had actually seen small deficits. The parish had virtually no savings or reserve. In a well-heeled community, we were a relatively poor parish.

☐ The physical plant was dirty and no longer functional in significant ways. Deferred maintenance seemed to be the maintenance plan. A surprising amount of useable space had been converted to storage space, although no one was sure what we were storing. The grounds were neglected and overgrown. The entrance looked as if the place were permanently closed.

☐ The small staff was divided and deeply dysfunctional. Their work was done in complete isolation from one another. They were a singularly unproductive group, but nearly everything that was done in the parish—from answering the phone to arranging the flowers—was done by them. Gossip and lunch were the only tasks they lent themselves to with enthusiasm. It should be noted, however, that they were paid next to nothing.

☐ Signs posted everywhere from some unidentified authority issued emphatic instructions always punctuated with exclamation points: "Keep these doors closed at all times!" "Do not move this table!!" "No lemons in the garbage disposal!!!"

☐ Bulletin boards and posters everywhere tried to attract parishioners' attention to everything from lost puppies to the latest fundraiser. As far as we know, no one even once paused to survey these posts. There was a weekly bulletin, but it was widely acknowledged that "no one reads it." So, most weekends it was read for them from the pulpit following communion. Perhaps that's why most people left after communion.

☐ The volunteers were a law unto themselves, answering to no one (except, perhaps, the former pastor). They included:

   1. *The ushers/money counters.* These men (there were no women) were the pastor's police force, invested with the responsibility of enforcing the pastor's house rules.
   2. *The religious education teachers.* Nobody really knew what these women (there were no men) did in their classrooms. And no one seemed to care either.
   3. *The cantors, lectors, and eucharistic ministers.* They had the job of sharing the spotlight with the celebrant and looking like the ultimate insiders.

☐ Clergy and staff were treated by parishioners as employees—sometimes with hostility, often with indifference, and, when we were doing what they wanted us to, with condescension.

☐ Complaint was a standard form of communication. Anything from failing to announce the Mass "intention" to the temperature inside the building would bring it on.

Inexplicably, there was a self-satisfied, self-congratulatory attitude the congregation as a whole seemed to share. Little else united them.

Besides the people who had been showing up for years, out of convenience or habit, the church was irrelevant and unknown in the community. The number one comment we heard in talking to people outside our congregation was, "I didn't know there was a church back there." A new nondenominational church in our neighborhood was meeting in a warehouse. It was half our age, twice our size, and growing. By their own acknowledgment, something like 60 percent of their congregation were former Catholics, including their pastor. As such, they were drawing more baptized Catholics than any Catholic church in north Baltimore.

These discoveries surprised and shocked us. But there was another little-known fact that was more shocking still: Our parish was dying. In what was already at that point a twenty-year pattern, between thirty and fifty people a year were literally dying or moving away, and nobody was replacing them.

Reflect and Resolve

1. Looking at the problems you checked off, prioritize the top three problems you believe must be addressed at your parish.

2. Which one do you think will be easiest to solve?

3. Which is going to be most difficult?

4. What's the most important problem you can address at this time? Write it down as simply as you can state it.

5. The team must now resolve to address this particular problem. Make sure everyone on the team embraces this resolution. What, specifically, are the next steps to be taken?

6. Who, particularly, is responsible for them?

7. When, exactly, is that going to happen? Set a next meeting date to report back.

Rally Cry

As a team, agree to take up the following rally cry:

> No matter what happens moving forward, we are going to be totally honest about our real problems.

This means,

> In appropriate ways, and always with charity, we resolve to acknowledge and discuss these problems and actively seek solutions.

Commit your rally cry to daily prayer. Ask God to stir in you a "holy discontent" about your rally cry; ask him to put it on your heart and help you serve it.

2

STOP DOING STUFF— ABSOLUTELY STOP

I am troubled now,
Yet what should I say?
"Father, save me from this hour"?
But it was for this purpose that I came to this hour.

JOHN 12:27

So what's our mission? That was exactly our problem. We were overwhelmed with the demands of our consumers and ignorant of our real mission. Until our trip to Rick Warren's church, we never even thought about it.

REBUILT, 38

PREPARE BY READING
Rebuilt: chapter 2 (pages 25–34) and chapter 3 (pages 37–39)

Consider

Did you ever have an experience where suddenly you ask, "Why am I here?" or "Why am I doing this?"

Sometimes it can happen at a party where we don't know many people and we feel out of place. Or we step into a situation and it's not what we thought it was going to be. It's a little uncomfortable. It happens in school a lot: you're sitting in class thinking, "Why am I here? I will never need this information." It's not really a big deal in small things, but it is hugely important to know our *why* in the more significant areas of life.

In the busyness of life, the *why* question usually doesn't get asked soon enough or often enough. We are usually running around instead, just trying to get through the day or complete our to-do lists. But answering the question *why* is vitally important.

It provides purpose and meaning; it adds value. The "why" question will get us through the difficult times and make the good times far more enjoyable. Knowing why you do what you do matters.

So why does the universal Church exist? Why does the local Church, which is our diocese, exist? Why does the very heart of the Church, which is our parish church, exist? And why do we do what we do there? With this step, you want to get crystal clear agreement on the purpose of the Church and evaluate how well you are staying focused on that mission in your parish.

Pray

Pray together. Begin in silent prayer; then add spontaneous prayers of thanksgiving and petition. Include prayer of intercession for clarity in your church's mission and vision. Then pray:

> Heavenly Father,
> in the days before he died, your Son faced the reality of the Cross
> and taught his disciples about the hope and promise it would hold.
> Despite whatever problems and challenges we face in our parish ministry,
> help us grow in our understanding of our mission
> and the purpose you call us to serve.
> We pray through Christ, our Lord.
> Amen.

Tell Your Story

In your own words,

Why was the parish founded?

Who originally established it, and what needs were they responding to?

What were they trying to accomplish?

Why does the parish *still* exist?

What is the purpose of your parish today and tomorrow?

Read Aloud

The following is excerpted and modified from Rebuilt, *pages 38–39. We suggest breaking the reading into parts and having more than one reader.*

Jesus actually gave the Church a clear mission, and he couldn't have been clearer. First came the "great command," two commands really, that he told us are more important than all the others. "You shall love the Lord, your God, with all your heart, with all your soul, and with all your mind. This is the greatest and the first commandment. The second is like it: You shall love your neighbor as yourself" (Mt 22:37–39).

And then, after his resurrection and before he ascended into heaven, he gathered the eleven apostles who still stood with him and gave them the Great Commission. "Go, therefore, and make disciples of all nations" (Mt 28:19).

Stop and Discuss: Jesus was very simple and completely clear about the mission he gave the Church. Why do you think it is so easy to forget this mission or lose sight of it?

Jesus, who suffered on the cross to regain the authority for humanity that our first parents had surrendered, passed on that authority to the apostles and their successors. And he told them what to do with it: love God and one another by making disciples. And in case they were wondering how many disciples to make or where, he was clear about that too: make disciples of everyone, everywhere.

The Church has a mission statement: make disciples. That's it.

Stop and Discuss: Does your parish actively reflect this mission? How?

Disciples are students. The Church is charged with shaping students for Jesus Christ. And like the owner in the parable of the talents (see Mt 25:24), he harvests where he has not sown and gathers where he has not scattered. In other words, he wants us to do it for him and like him. He modeled it for us when he walked the earth.

Reflect and Resolve

1. Take a look at your bulletin or other church communication. If you were an outsider looking at these announcements, what would you assume is the mission of your parish?

2. Have each team member, by themselves, go through the bulletin, website, or weekly pulpit announcements and mark every event focused on making disciples. Be honest. Be brutally honest.

3. Now, discuss your answers with the rest of the group and share notes. How well did you do?

4. If your team is serious about making disciples and reaching the unchurched in your community, it is vitally important that you free up your staff time, volunteer efforts, and available resources to make it happen. Is the team actually committed to this principle?

5. What do you need to stop doing at your church or in your parish ministry because it clearly does not serve the mission to make disciples? Make a list. Now, decide which event, activity, or program on that list you are going to kill (here's a hint: it's probably a fundraiser), who is going to do the dirty deed, and when. Set a date for your next team meeting to report back on progress. After your initial success, decide what's next.

Rally Cry

As a team, decide to take up the following rally cry:

> We will absolutely stop doing things that are not serving the mission and purpose of this parish.

This means,

> Instead, we'll focus our efforts and resources for the greatest impact in serving the kingdom of God in our generation.

Commit your cry to prayer. Ask God to stir in you a "holy discontent" about your rally cry; ask him to put it on your heart and help you serve it.

3
FIND TIM

[Jesus said,] "For the Son of Man has come to seek and to save what was lost."

LUKE 19:10

Jesus made lost people his priority. And he went out of his way (way, way out of his way) to do it. He spent time where they spent time. He knew how to talk to them and what was important to them. He recognized their worries, fears, sorrows, and sins. He understood their hearts, and he loved them by making an investment in them. Jesus found lost people and then he made them disciples.

REBUILT, 40

PREPARE BY READING
Rebuilt: chapter 3 (pages 40–48) and chapter 5 (pages 71–76)

Consider

People far from God were a priority for Jesus. He called them the "lost." But what is it about churchworld that we tend to drift so far away from this core mission of our Savior? Without intentionally focusing on the lost, Church culture tends to get lost itself. We focus on ourselves instead, quickly becoming consumer exchanges often antagonistic toward the lost.

Rebuilding your parish, becoming the Church Christ wants, requires a laser-like focus on the lost. The purpose of this step is to help you describe the lost in your community as a first movement toward gaining that focus.

Pray

Pray in silence as a team. Include a prayer of intercession for all the lost people in your community. Then have someone read the following aloud:

> [Jesus] came to Jericho and intended to pass through the town. Now a man there named Zacchaeus, who was a chief tax collector and also a wealthy man, was seeking to see who Jesus was; but he could not see him because of the crowd, for he was short in stature.
>
> So he ran ahead and climbed a sycamore tree in order to see Jesus, who was about to pass that way. When he reached the place, Jesus looked up and said to him, "Zacchaeus, come down quickly, for today I must stay at your house."
>
> And he came down quickly and received him with joy. When they all saw this, they began to grumble, saying, "He has gone to stay at the house of a sinner." But Zacchaeus stood there and said to the Lord, "Behold, half of my possessions, Lord, I shall give to the poor, and if I have extorted anything from anyone I shall repay it four times over."
>
> And Jesus said to him, "Today salvation has come to this house because this man too is a descendant of Abraham. For the Son of Man has come to seek and to save what was lost."
>
> LUKE 19:1–10

Then pray:

> Heavenly Father,
> in coming to seek and save the lost,
> your Son found the thief and traitor Zacchaeus,
> changing his life forever and making him a disciple.
> Break our hearts for those who are far from you.
> Shape us into a parish that will go out of our way
> to reach them.
> May the lost in our community come to know Christ
> because of the work of this team.

We pray through Christ, our Lord.
Amen.

Tell Your Story

Talk about your own family and friends who don't go to church. What happened? When and why did they stop going?

Read Aloud

The following is excerpted and modified from Rebuilt, *pages 45–46. We suggest breaking the reading into parts and having more than one reader.*

Sure, lost people might be shallow and unsure in their faith. They are not going to appreciate our procedures and practices, nor are they contributing members yet. But, at some level, these people are seeking God. And if we don't help them find him, not only are they lost, but also we are too.

The Church of the Nativity was never even in the business of reaching the lost. It was irrelevant to the lost. And we wanted to be that way. We were proud that we were that way. In fact, we blamed the lost for being lost. It was somehow their fault. They deserved to be lost because they weren't interested in doing church our way. Incidentally, Jesus never blamed the lost for being lost; he just wanted to find them. As long as we ignored his example and held onto our own views, we were abdicating our spiritual leadership. And we'd lost our mission.

Of course, you cannot turn your church upside down every time someone new comes in the door or abandon your values to try to please everyone. Certainly every congregation has a serious responsibility to care for its members and hold to high standards when it comes to the sacraments. That is not being questioned. But many churches not only care for members but also coddle them. They pander their demands and expectations. And then they turn around and challenge the outsiders.

That's backward. We should be attractive and accessible to outsiders and challenging to insiders, helping them to change and move beyond consumerism to growth as disciples.

Reflect and Resolve

1. Define your mission field. What is the zip code (or zip codes) of your parish?

2. Find out how many people live in your parish boundaries. What are the demographics of the community?

3. Is there anything about your community that is unique or distinctive? (For example, Portland, Oregon, boasts lots of outdoor enthusiasts.) Do the majority of people work in a certain industry or field? (Austin, Texas, is a sophisticated, academically centered community.) Are people drawn together by a certain interest? (Green Bay, Wisconsin, is a huge football town.) Does your town have a predominant religious affiliation? (The majority of people in north Baltimore are culturally Catholic.)

4. How do people spend their time? How do they spend their money? What role do sports play when it comes to leisure time and disposable income? Where do the kids go to school? Where do parishioners shop? Begin to compile a list of the defining characteristics of your community's culture. Develop as complete an understanding of that culture as you can.

5. Most research indicates that only about 20 percent of the general population in the United States attends church "regularly" (two times a month). Let's assume that is also true of your community. The remaining 80 percent are the lost you're seeking. But as long as that 80 percent remains a number, your efforts at evangelization will never be very dynamic. Nothing is ever dynamic until it is specific.

In *Rebuilt*, we discussed the quintessential unchurched person in our community. Being in Timonium, Maryland, we called him "Tim" (yeah, as in "Timonium Tim"). It's kind of cute and kind of annoying, but it is easy to remember, and here's the thing: rarely a weekend goes by that someone doesn't approach us to say, "Hi, I'm Tim."

Now comes the fun part. Define your Tim. Each member of the team can create a description of the quintessential unchurched guy (or gal) in your community. Afterward, compare notes and see if the team can come up with a single someone. Give your guy a name. Be sure to talk about Tim's worries and fears, as well as his "felt" needs, those things he *thinks* he needs. What does he believe adds meaning and value to his life? Compile a list of what Tim does on Sunday morning instead of going to church. If you don't know, find out. Send team members out into the community at peak Mass times to see what else is going on.

6. After you have defined your lost person, put it into a document and send it out to all staff members and volunteer leaders. Invite their input. As your team continues its work, keep coming back to your profile and refining it.

Meanwhile, consider this: there is plenty of data easily available that tells us why the unchurched don't go to church. Typically, the number one reason given is that they don't feel welcome. So if Tim actually showed up at your church, how welcome would he be? Go ahead and give yourself a grade. Often, the number two reason given is that they consider church boring and irrelevant. If Tim decided to give your church a try, how relevant would the experience be? Give yourself a grade.

Perhaps the third most-cited reason unchurched people stop going to church is because the church is all about religious rule keeping rather than personal growth. Give yourself a grade on that too.

Rally Cry

As a team, agree to take up the following rally cry:

> Moving forward, our parish is, first and foremost, all about [add your Tim's name].

This means,

> We are going to plan with him in mind; we're going to more and more get away from what does not work when it comes to evangelization and discipleship for the unchurched in our community. We will begin shaping environments and attitudes to welcome them, and we'll start praying for them too. Finally, we will commit to care about all our communication and how it speaks to the lost.

Commit your rally cry to daily prayer. Ask God to stir in you a "holy discontent" about your rally cry; ask him to put it on your heart and help you serve it.

4
WORK WEEKENDS

Martha, burdened with much serving, came to him and said, "Lord, do you not care that my sister has left me by myself to do the serving? Tell her to help me." The Lord said to her in reply, "Martha, Martha, you are anxious and worried about many things. There is need of only one thing. Mary has chosen the better part and it will not be taken from her."

LUKE 10:40–42

The weekend experience is the number one opportunity for people in the community to connect with church. And almost everyone who actually does come in contact with the parish does so on the weekend. In that brief time, they will decide if it's worth it to come back or not. If the experience is boring and bad, then they won't.

REBUILT, 90–91

PREPARE BY READING
Rebuilt: chapter 6 (pages 87–93)

Consider

Imagine yourself in a restaurant where the wait staff is indifferent, perhaps even hostile, to you, the plates and cutlery are dirty, and the food is terrible. Would it really matter to you that their accounting system was excellent or that their recent renovation was really beautiful? Of course not.

The "weekend experience" is what we've come to call the sum total of people's time on our campus during that narrow window, when visitors are likely to visit. The work of the parish really is all about this. And it is just amazing to us how this basic point is missed over and over (and over and over) again.

The weekend experience is basic to *who* we are; it is *what* we do. If we don't get this piece right when it comes to evangelization, everything else we do might just be wasted effort (or worse, counterproductive). Think about it: if we're getting people back to church only to remind them of why they stopped going to begin with, we could be doing more harm than good. And unfortunately, if their experience of our church is boring and bad, they can come to view the Gospel, and even God himself, in that way too.

The weekend experience is crucial for evangelization and discipleship. It is the key tool for reaching unchurched people and getting them onto the discipleship path. It's also the primary, essential place you are growing disciples. The culture of your church is fundamentally shaped by what happens on the weekend. So, it is critical that your team begin to create momentum in improving what you're doing. In this step, you will evaluate your weekend experience and decide some next steps to improve it.

Pray

Pray together. Begin in silent prayer and then add spontaneous prayers of thanksgiving and petition. Include prayer of intercession for your weekend experience and all who currently serve there. Then pray:

> Heavenly Father,
> you led your faithful disciple Martha to even greater discipleship
> through the example of her sister's worship.
> Help us use our time, talent, and treasure to better serve you
> and make disciples through an ever more excellent
> weekend experience at our parish.
> We pray this through Christ, our Lord.
> Amen.

Tell Your Story

Discuss together your weekend experience. Try to be honest about the whole of it. Who is involved, what do they do, and how much preparation is involved? What is the basic budget for the weekend, and how does it compare to the rest of your expenses?

Read Aloud

The following is excerpted and modified from Rebuilt, *pages 92–93. We suggest breaking the reading into parts and having more than one reader.*

Let's be honest. Many of the people coming to church these days do not understand the Mass and are simply not engaged in it. And all the cultural Catholics in our community, who aren't even showing up, have simply walked away from the Eucharist entirely. They have tuned the Church out, and no matter how beautifully or faithfully we celebrate this sacrament—and we should celebrate it beautifully and faithfully—it's not getting them back. The sad irony we have found in discussion with former Catholics who have decamped to evangelical churches is their nearly uniform explanation, "I just felt like I wasn't being fed."

To begin to reverse this situation in our community, we started looking beyond the Liturgy of the Eucharist to the elements of the weekend experience that could have the greatest impact on the dechurched and those new to the discipleship path. We have been criticized and mischaracterized on this point so we want to be clear. The Eucharist is central to our parish and our weekend worship. What we are talking about is simply acknowledging where people are and meeting them where they are in order to lead them more effectively and successfully into a fuller appreciation and celebration of the Eucharist.

Reflect and Resolve

Each team member should take time to evaluate the parish on the basics of the weekend experience.

1. What is your weekend schedule? Do you have too many Masses? Which ones could be eliminated or consolidated?

2. What is the experience approaching your church? How's the parking? Signage? Accessibility?

3. Consider the physical setting: What about cleanliness and lack of clutter? How well can people see and hear? What is the experience of lighting like?

4. Which staff and volunteer ministers work weekends, and what are they doing? How well are they doing it, and what training do they receive? What accountability do they have?

5. What is the experience for children? What is the experience for parents with small children? The music? The preaching? (Be honest.)

6. What is the quality of other forms of weekend communication, such as the bulletin or the announcements?

7. How's your hospitality? Is there any form of fellowship in your weekend experience?

8. What preparation goes into the weekend experience? And what evaluation is ever made about this experience?

Now, compare notes and try to come to consensus about your grading. Take some time to discuss strengths, weaknesses, and opportunities for growth.

Prioritize the top three issues that your team can begin to address in the short term.

Rally Cry

As a team, agree to take up the following rally cry:

> Our parish is going to prioritize the weekend experience over everything else we do.

This means,

> We are going to work weekends with a special view to the experience of the unchurched.

Commit your rally cry to daily prayer. Ask God to stir in you a "holy discontent" about your rally cry; ask him to put it on your heart and help you serve it.

5

FAST AND PRAY FOR MUSIC

Sing to him a new song; skillfully play.

PSALM 33:3

The weekend experience should be a form of transportation, taking the participant on an emotional, intellectual, and ultimately spiritual journey to the higher things of God. . . . We like to say that music is the water on which the experience sails. More than any other element in the church's weekend experience, it is the music that can touch and change people's hearts—for better or for worse.

REBUILT, 93–94

PREPARE BY READING

Rebuilt: chapter 6 (pages 93–105)

Consider

After air temperature, music is the single greatest environmental factor for your community, because it determines how people *feel* in your church. Music has the ability to move people in the deepest part of their souls in a way nothing else can. Regardless of someone's beliefs, music can speak directly to the heart. It will always leave an impression, even if we do not completely understand or know the words. Music moves us.

And yet, despite the almost limitless impression and impact music can make, it is often neglected. When we share the problems and pain we have had with music at our parish, audiences howl with laughter because the experiences resonate deeply. Music will be the greatest challenge you will face in prioritizing the weekend, creating an environment that reaches the lost and puts members of your church on the path to discipleship. The temptation will be to leave it alone or just let it go because it is so fraught with egos and emotions, a minefield of personal preferences and intractable positions. But don't ignore this one. Music matters in winning souls and making disciples of Jesus Christ. It matters a lot.

Music has such an incredible influence on the soul that approaching it as a project is really a spiritual battle. We have come to believe you cannot make any progress on your music without prayer coupled with fasting. Fasting and prayer prepare us for spiritual victories. As you go through this chapter, contemplate how your team can fast and pray for the music so you can make great strides.

Pray

Pray in silence as a team. Remember to pray for your music ministers, past, present, and yet to come. Then pray aloud (a single leader or as a group):

> Heavenly Father,
> you have given us the gift of music.
> We praise and thank you for the power music has beyond our understanding.
> Through this exercise may we come to know
> how you want to use music in our community,
> so that the lost will connect with you and members will grow as disciples.
> Help us to go where you are blessing.
> We pray this through Christ, our Lord.
> Amen.

Tell Your Story

What music "spoke" to you in your youth? Which musical experiences have connected you to God and helped form you as a disciple of Jesus Christ? Is there a particular hymn or song now that resonates with you? What kind of music do you prefer at Mass? (You may as well get that one out on the table.)

Read Aloud

The following is excerpted and modified from Rebuilt, *pages 101–104. We suggest breaking the reading into parts and having more than one reader.*

We are *not* advocating any particular style of music. In the multicultural reality that is American Catholicism, that would be absurd. Besides, in Catholic worship the *Novus Ordo* can accommodate many different musical styles as long as the music fulfills three basic criteria as outlined by Pope Benedict XVI:

It is related to God's Word and *"God's saving action."*

It lifts the human heart toward God.

It more effectively unites the individual with the larger community.

Beyond that, it's about discovering the music that works in your community—not the personal preferences of the pastor or the music director (often not exactly identical anyway), not the demands from the pews, and not even the stated preferences of the majority. The music must be all about attracting the lost and growing disciples through worship.

Stop and Discuss: What are the strongest aspects of your music program? Where is it weakest? What are your musical values as a parish?

We try to make sure the music is connected to the liturgical action. There must be direction and flow to it, contoured to the ritual itself. Just as the liturgical year brings what has been called "progressive solemnity" (that is, some feasts call for greater or more solemn celebration), the same can be said for the Mass itself. Inherent in the celebration of the Eucharist is a progressive solemnity, and it can be powerfully underscored with music. For our community and in our culture, we think music at the entrance rite should communicate a feel of arrival, perhaps even urgency, drawing people into an "event" experience. Music at the offertory can begin to lead people deeper into the mystery of the Eucharist itself. At Communion, softer or more poignant music can be truly uplifting and inspiring. The closing should be a high-energy send-off.

Stop and Discuss: What is the process for your selection of music? How can this be improved so that your music reflects your values?

To get where you need to go isn't about talent, luck, or even money. It's about consistently following a few basic principles:

- Make sure you have the best musicians you can find (paid or volunteer) and use them. Treat them well too. Do the difficult thing and ask people who are holding your program down or even making it worse to step aside. Face the hard facts, and lean into the conflict in order to advance your program.
- Raise your music and musicians up in prayer. Fast for them. Form a program for fasting: making Fridays meatless, giving up desserts, skipping meals.
- Regardless of the style, make sure your music is worship and your musicians are worship leaders.
- Take care with the selection of your music, and do it in view of the liturgy as well as the lost. You need to be talking to your musicians about the music. It's not about what you like or they want; it's about the unchurched.
- Don't be afraid to repeat music from week to week. In loving ways, encourage your congregation to sing, and sing with them.

Reflect and Resolve

1. What type of music do the people in your community listen to? Does the music at your church in any way reflect their preferences?

2. Are the musicians skilled and competent, or do they struggle in basic skills? Do your musicians have the right "heart"? Do they bring a worshipful heart and a spirit of service, or are they in performance mode? What type of prayer and fasting could you undertake for the benefit of your music?

3. What is one way you can invest relationally in the musicians of your parish?

4. From the above list of basic principles about music, what do you think would be the most effective in improving music at Mass?

5. Does anyone need to step down in order for your program to move forward?

Rally Cry

As a team, agree to take up the following rally cry:

> We commit to a program of prayer and fasting on behalf of our music program.

This means,

> We pray God will help us understand what it is we are to do and grant us the courage to do it.

Commit your rally cry to daily prayer. Ask God to stir in you a "holy discontent" about your rally cry; ask him to put it on your heart and help you serve it.

6

BECOME A CHURCH FOR THE UNCHURCHED

And he gave some as apostles, others as prophets, others as evangelists, others as pastors and teachers, to equip the holy ones for the work of ministry, for building up the body of Christ.

EPHESIANS 4:11–12

I was . . . a stranger and you welcomed me.

MATTHEW 25:35

Focusing on the weekend from the perspective of lost people means . . . "It's all about the ministers!" We're definitely not interested in pandering to the consumer demands of members, because we don't want them to remain consumers. But that's where people start. So, we do want to engage our potential members by offering an attractive and accessible weekend experience. Our parishioners who serve as volunteer ministers remove some of the obstacles and make that happen. Little things can get in the way. If you can't find a parking spot, don't feel

welcomed, or sit in a dirty pew, it can be difficult to
focus on God. Little things become big things.

Rebuilt, 106

PREPARE BY READING
Rebuilt: chapter 6 (pages 105–113), chapter 7, and chapter 11

Consider

As a Church, we are charged to influence people who are far from God with the life-changing message of Jesus Christ. Much of that message runs counter to the way our culture thinks and acts. Much of it also runs contrary to our fallen human nature. And yet, God calls us to use that message to influence our culture and community. Acceptance paves the way to influence. We will listen to people who accept and love us.

Churches naturally focus their efforts and attention on insiders and sometimes ignore outsiders, or worse. As early as the Council of Jerusalem (ca. AD 50), there were religious leaders who wanted to make it difficult for the outsiders to become members of the Church—difficult as in painful: they wanted circumcision to be the entry price. If that view had prevailed, it is easy to imagine Christianity remaining a very small sect (not to mention a weird one).

If left untended, perhaps unintentionally, your parish culture will become unwelcoming and unaccepting of outsiders. It's just what happens in churchworld. That's why volunteers in your parish—we call them member ministers—are so important. Parishioners who serve one another are ministers in the true sense of the word (ie, servants). And beyond any specific task they may undertake, they are critical in changing the consumer, me-first culture of many parishes. Volunteer ministers lead the cultural change your parish needs to become a church for outsiders. In addition, member ministers create a sense of excitement and welcome for visitors. And they set the tone for the weekend experience because they are the first point of contact on your campus.

In this step, we will look at some of the key ministries needed to create a great weekend experience for the unchurched. It's also about evaluating those ministries with an eye toward constantly improving them.

Pray

Pray together. Begin in silent prayer and then add spontaneous prayers of thanksgiving and petition. Pray for your current parishioners, and for a change in their hearts. Pray for the lost in your community, that they open their hearts. Then pray:

> Heavenly Father,
> while we were still sinners, you sent your Son to die for us.
> You accepted us when we could do nothing for you.
> Create within the hearts of our parishioners a love for the lost.
> Inspire them to serve as your Son served us.
> Help us to raise up volunteer ministers in our weekend experience
> who communicate your great love for all your children.
> Lead the lost back to the Church.
> We pray this through Christ, our Lord.
> Amen.

Tell Your Story

Where is a place you received excellent service or hospitality: a hotel, a friend's home, a shopping or entertainment venue? What feelings did that experience evoke? What about the opposite experience? Tell about a time when you felt unnoticed or unwelcomed.

Read Aloud

The following is excerpted and modified from Rebuilt, *pages 106–107, 117–121, and 198–201. We suggest breaking the reading into parts and having more than one reader.*

In our community, people tend to bring their cars with them when they come to church. So we've got to take care of their cars before we can take care of them. For us, the whole weekend experience and all our ministry efforts begin with our Parking Team. They direct traffic, manage flow, assist with special needs, and make sure we're accommodating the maximum number of cars. But more importantly, our parking ministry is also about establishing a welcoming, festive environment as people enter our campus, wordlessly communicating, "We're waiting for you. We're glad you're here."

Once inside the building, our Host Team adds words to the welcome. Their goal is to greet everyone who comes through any of our doors, demonstrating in a convincing way our enthusiasm for their presence with us. There is nothing quite as welcoming as people who are happy to see you.

At this point in their experience, guests are probably smiling, and we've already begun to successfully preach the gospel. We've worked our way out of the old idea of ushers and promoted hosts as aides who assist and accommodate guests. But hosts are also charged with performing the tasks formerly associated with the ushers, like taking up the offering. They're also on hand to "control" the house. The attractive environment we're aiming to have will only happen if it's a *controlled* environment, free of disruptions. The Host Team has a plan for greeting and seating, but whatever they're doing, hopefully they are shaping an environment in which adults and young adults can get some distance from the rest of their lives, relax, and focus on God.

Besides directional questions, the Host Team doesn't try to answer all the questions; the Information Team does. Stationed in the lobby with their own desk and laptop, they handle—you guessed it—information. The team provides visitors with details about programs and services, and helps members sign up to take their next steps in discipleship.

Often, people in our culture circle back around to church when they have children. They realize how difficult it is to be a parent. They are searching for help in this new challenge of raising children, an authority greater than themselves. Perhaps it is all about the culture of religion more than faith, but we can use this opportunity to draw them into a relationship with their Savior if we provide accessible programs.

Our hospitality ministries for adults are matched with programs for children. One of the major reasons unchurched people say they don't like church is because they feel their children are unwelcome. And they *feel* that way because their children *are* unwelcome. At least noisy, disruptive children are unwelcome, and kids at certain ages inevitably become disruptive in a sixty-minute service incomprehensible to them.

One of the best strategic decisions we ever made was to begin to build weekend programs to better accommodate our youngest parishioners and make the weekend experience better for the whole family.

There are certainly lots of ways to approach this opportunity. Currently we offer the following programs:

> *Kidzone*: Programs for our youngest members, six months to age three, start in what we call "kidzone." We just want to make sure church is a place where they're known and loved, a place they love to visit. But it's not babysitting; there's worship music and a gospel-based message.

> *All Stars*: Three-to-six-year-olds go here. We call it a "play-worship-learn" environment, offering a program reflecting the pattern of the liturgy. Children gather for fun and fellowship, participate in worship, hear a presentation of the day's gospel, and end with a snack.

> *Time Travelers*: For grades one through five we call our children's Liturgy of the Word program "Time Travelers" because we think that sounds more interesting to kids. We want

them to get to know the story of the Bible, often by introducing them to costumed biblical characters. In just this way, we want them to come to understand that the Word of God is alive and that they can live that Word.

Along with the required safety and compliance procedures, all of our ministers for adults and children's programs are asked to agree to our ministry values and standards. There are lots of ways to approach such statements. Here's our current take.

Ministry Values

As you read these ministry values, check the ones you want to see played out in the volunteer ministries of your parish.

First Value: Ministers recognize that they are working for God. Besides praying as a team, our members are asked to approach their service prayerfully and see themselves as servants of the Lord.

Second Value: Ministers work together in teams and maintain clear, respectful communication with their teammates and leaders.

Third Value: Ministers share a common sense of purpose, recognizing that, in some specific way, what they are doing is serving our church-wide purpose. There is no unimportant ministry, no matter how modest or simple the task; it's all in service to reaching the lost and making disciples.

Fourth Value: Ministers are sensitive to physical and emotional obstacles, and real or imagined roadblocks that prevent guests from having a great experience and parishioners going deeper. They take pride in a clean, attractive environment that minimizes distractions from the church-wide message.

Fifth Value: Ministers aim at shaping environments that are reliably excellent; they share best practices and work to continue to raise the standard of our service.

Ministry Standards

As you read these ministry standards, think about how you might adapt them to your own parish. Discuss your ideas together once you finish reading the list.

Show up for ministry: Just because they're working for free doesn't mean ministers can take a day off whenever they want, come late and leave early, or serve according to their own rules.

Minister casually: We're deliberately trying to create a casual environment in which the lost in our community will feel comfortable. Our ministers reflect that, dressing in a way that matches how the lost in our community show up for church (smart casual), many others wear distinctive shirts, T-shirts, vests, or aprons as a sign of their service.

Minister prepared: Ministers need to know what's going on at the parish. An in-week e-mail updates them on the weekend message so they are fully informed.

Minister and worship: Ministry is not what you do at Mass. It's not an alternative to worship. Disciples do both.

Minister to win: Ministers need to know what ministry wins are and we need to give them opportunities to celebrate them.

Reflect and Resolve

1. What grade would you give the hospitality of your parish? Is it a welcoming place?

2. Of the ministries listed previously, which would be the easiest to get going or improve in your parish?

3. How can you make it easy and accessible for people to get involved and stay involved?

4. How should you communicate your ministry values and standards to the volunteer ministers in your parish?

5. How can you consistently and effectively communicate your values and standards to all your members as well as your ministers?

Rally Cry

As a team, agree to take up the following rally cry:

> We reject a church culture of consumerism.

This means,

> We are going to begin to challenge our congregation to help shape a welcoming, hospitable parish through accessible ministry structures.

Commit your rally cry to daily prayer. Ask God to stir in you a "holy discontent" about your rally cry; ask him to put it on your heart and help you serve it.

7

MAKE THE
MESSAGE MATTER

So the Twelve called together the community of the
disciples and said, "It is not right for us to neglect the
word of God to serve at table. . . . We shall devote
ourselves to prayer and to the ministry of the word."

ACTS 6:2, 4

Words have power, and God's words have God's
power.

REBUILT, 138

PREPARE BY READING
Rebuilt: chapter 8

Consider

As you think back on your life, reflect on the amazing impact words have had. Perhaps words were spoken that wounded you. Perhaps you may have been bullied or harassed, or given a certain name that hurt your heart. On the other hand, you may remember just the right word of encouragement that helped you to get through a difficult time or overcome a daunting obstacle. Words have power. Words matter.

Words matter in every area of our lives, including our spiritual lives. As you think back on your faith life, you can probably remember a time when words moved you closer to God and the Church. Maybe you used to think of God as a cosmic cop just waiting to catch you breaking the law, but then someone explained that God is your heavenly Father who sent his Son to die for you. And hearing those words completely changed your relationship with God.

Maybe words have altered your position on a moral issue. You bought some lie the culture was peddling and just thought God and the Church were wrong. Then you heard the issue explained in a loving, Christ-like way, and those words totally changed your view.

Words have power. They matter. Yet, when working on a homily or parish presentation, we are not sure our efforts are making an impact. Perhaps it can even feel as if we're wasting our time and energy.

This is possibly the reason that in Catholic culture, little value is sometimes placed on the homily. That has to change. The pulpit is the rudder of the ship that is your parish, which should be shaping all your parish communication. If you are going to change the culture in your church, the quality of your preaching must be carefully considered. In this exercise, the team will examine your attitude toward the weekend homilies and how to make the message matter.

Pray

Pray together. Begin in silent prayer and then add spontaneous prayers of thanksgiving and petition. Pray for those who serve the ministry of the word in your parish. Pray for your preachers, teachers, and lectors. Then pray:

> Heavenly Father,
> you spoke the world into existence
> and through your word created the heavens and the earth.
> Your word is effective and holds the power to rebuild.
> Through this exercise, may we come to know
> how you want to use your word to change and transform
> the members of our church and reach the lost.
> We pray this through Christ, our Lord.
> Amen.

Tell Your Story

What words of encouragement have been spoken into your life? What was going on in your life at the time? Can you remember a homily or teaching that significantly impacted your relationship with God?

What's the best homily you have heard in the last year at your parish? What's the best homily you've ever heard? What made them effective?

Read Aloud

The following material is excerpted and modified from Rebuilt, *pages 140–146. We suggest breaking the reading into parts and having more than one reader.*

Here's the key: in a setting like Church of the Nativity, we were too often speaking only from our own authority. We weren't really relying on God's authority. And in the process we were limiting our effectiveness and our church growth. In looking at the most successful churches in the country, we discovered that their approach was very different from ours, and we began to challenge and change some of our assumptions.

The principles we now rely on are listed below. As you read the list, ask yourself which principles your parish strongly embodies and which ones you think your parish could more effectively embrace.

1. *Preach to yourself:* Prayer should be foundational to all preaching and preparation for preaching. At the same time, and if you're actually trying to apply what you preach to your own life, your preaching will always be authentic. The first life that should be changed by your preaching is your own. Your preaching must come out of your lived experience of trying to walk with God, learning from him, and being transformed into his image. That's why preaching and preparation for preaching should find its foundation in prayer.

2. *Preach to your community:* In the same vein, we have to be very deliberate about preaching to our people. Preaching to the community means we need to connect with our community on several levels. Aristotle noted that when someone is speaking, an audience determines whether or not they will listen to the speaker based on *ethos, logos,* and *pathos.* Ethos asks questions like, "Are you ethical?" or "Are you telling the truth?" As preachers, our lives need to be transparently authentic if anybody is going to listen to us. *Logos* asks, "Do you know what you are talking about?" As preachers, we must base our message in God's word and the Church's Magisterium to answer this question successfully. *Pathos* asks the question, "Do you care about me?" or "Are you speaking in my best interest?" To answer this question, we're going to have to know our community and how to connect with them emotionally. Overlooking the emotional connection of a message will cause people to shut down and turn the message off.

   Effectively engaging the emotional content of the congregation's life will take work, because it's about entering other people's worlds and working from the perspective of their experience. Arguably the most important and powerful element in making an emotional connection with an audience is through humor: not jokes, not comedy, and not camp, but definitely making people laugh. When they laugh they relax . . . and listen.

3. *Preach one message*: Around here it is axiomatic to say, "one church, one message." We work hard to try to offer the same message at every weekend Mass.

4. *Preach messages in series*: A "message series" is about exploring a single theme over the course of multiple weekends. This is a common practice in the evangelical churches we have studied. But if you think about it, the idea makes so much more sense in liturgical churches that have the liturgy's seasons and the lectionary's cycles of readings. It is interesting to explore the themes that are woven through the Church year in our series. Preaching in series makes preaching prep easier, because we're not starting with a blank slate every week. It also encourages people to keep coming back to hear the rest of the message. And it helps the message to more effectively sink in.

5. *Preach the purpose of the message*: Preach life change. Augustine said teach and engage in order to change people, to help them move intellectually and emotionally from where they are to where God wants them to be.

6. *Preach the outcomes of the message*: What, specifically, do you want them to change? What is the message, and what do you want them to do with that message? Aim at nothing and you will hit every time. Aim at something instead.

7. *Preach the announcements*: We have come to include church-wide goals in our message series, asking the question, "How will the church be different after than before?"

8. *Preach other people's messages*: Plagiarism is a serious ethical violation. But it is not plagiarism to avail yourself of the tremendous resources that other preachers out there are only too happy to share. As Rick Warren says, "We're all on the same team." Reading and listening to the messages other preachers make available for this purpose can be a great way to grow your repertoire; not copying or aping but adopting available material and making it your own.

9. *Preach prepared*: If you consistently step into the pulpit only after rock-solid preparation, if your congregation can go to the bank on your preparation, and if they know they can invite friends and will not be disappointed, you will have their attention. You won't need attention getters to try to trick them into paying attention to you. People notice when you put time and energy into your message, and they will appreciate it.

10. *Preach God's word*: Make sure it is all about the Word of God and nothing else. When we are faithful to the Word of God, relevancy follows naturally.

Reflect and Resolve

1. In what ways is the typical weekend homily strongest? In what ways is it weak?

2. Is there a consistency to the homilies heard at your parish each weekend, or are there conflicting messages from Mass to Mass or time to time?

3. What are the obstacles to having the same message, or at least consistent messages at every Mass?

4. Do your preachers, presenters, and lectors have the skill to speak and present? Is there a speaker who needs to practice a great deal more before preaching on a weekend or who should stop speaking altogether?

Rally Cry

As a team, agree to take up the following rally cry:

> We will devote resources and effort to support those who preach at our weekend Masses.

This means,

> We will work for ways to help coordinate one church/one message. We will look for ways to widen the reach of the weekend message through other forms of parish communication.

Commit your rally cry to daily prayer. Ask God to stir in you a "holy discontent" about your rally cry; ask him to put it on your heart and help you serve it.

8

CHALLENGE CHURCHPEOPLE

They devoted themselves to the teaching of the apostles and to the communal life, to the breaking of the bread and to the prayers. Awe came upon everyone, and many wonders and signs were done through the apostles. All who believed were together and had all things in common; they would sell their property and possessions and divide them among all according to each one's need. Every day they devoted themselves to meeting together in the temple.... They ate their meals with exultation and sincerity of heart, praising God and enjoying favor with all the people. And every day the Lord added to their number.

ACTS 2:42–47

Over a period of just a couple of years our thinking and feelings did a complete about face when it came to our perspective on doing church. We more or less resolved to challenge the status quo and change the culture. We started deliberately doing things differently. And the main difference was in

focus. We were going to start challenging churchpeople and seeking lost people.

Rebuilt, 48

PREPARE BY READING
Rebuilt: chapters 9 and 10

Consider

We all come to Jesus out of neediness. That is no different than the men and women we meet in the gospels. People came to him because he taught brilliantly and told fascinating and funny stories. They came to Jesus for healing and health. They came to him out of some felt need or simple self-interest. Many who came to him did so only for the free food. Even the apostles followed Jesus out of a selfish ambition: they wanted to be large and in charge in the coming royal reign they assumed was inevitable. Jesus didn't turn away people who were coming to him to meet their needs. He used those opportunities to meet their needs and *then* he challenged them to grow in faith. The problem in our churches is not that people *come to us* as consumers. The problem is that they *remain* consumers for five, ten, twenty, or forty years, and for many, a whole lifetime long. They're only with us to meet an obligation, or because church contributes to their vision of an ideal family life. Perhaps they're just coming to indulge in self-absorbed spiritual comfort. Our role as spiritual leaders is to meet people exactly where they are and take them on a journey of faith. We are to move them from mere religious consumers to ever more fully devoted followers who are *contributors*.

We must challenge them out of the consumer mentality in two ways. We call it going deeper *and* wider. First, we've got to challenge them to take on the responsibility to grow in faith by developing a personal, intimate relationship with Jesus Christ. Second, the challenge is to invest them with personal responsibility for the mission of the Church by joining us in making disciples.

As Acts of the Apostles shows, when you can get people to contribute their time and resources to the Church and, in the process, forget about their own needs, it creates an unmatched spiritual energy and momentum. Church health and growth inevitably follow. In this step, we will look at how to challenge churchpeople so that more and more of them can experience real life change.

Pray

Pray together. Begin in silent prayer and then add spontaneous prayers of thanksgiving and petition. Remember in prayer the people of your congregation. Perhaps even bring along a registry of parishioners and name some of them, in the style of a litany. Then pray:

> Heavenly Father,
> your Son challenged the insiders and comforted outsiders.
> Help us to learn from him.
> Strengthen us to touch and change the hearts of the people in our pews
> to take ownership of their faith
> and accept responsibility for the mission to go and make disciples.
> Give us wisdom to lead and serve as you command.
> We pray through Christ, our Lord.
> Amen.

Tell Your Story

Share your own faith journey. What environments, relationships, or practices were crucial to your becoming a follower of Christ? At what point did you decide to get up out of the pews and start serving? What, or who, motivated you?

Read Aloud

The following material is adapted from Rebuilt. *We suggest breaking the reading into parts and having more than one reader.*

Discipleship is all about simple steps. When we know what those steps are, we can more reliably take our parishioners where we want them to go and get there faster. And when we've got partners on the path, the journey is less difficult. In a certain sense, just being around other people who are even trying to live the Christian life will make the effort easier. As spiritual leaders, we are to shape the path of discipleship for the people in our pews and set up environments and opportunities so followers of Christ move together in the same direction.

To shape a path and set a direction for spiritual growth, clarity about the steps we want people to take is important. Our challenges must be specific and consistent if we are to effectively move parishioners from consumers to contributors to leaders in rebuilding the parish.

Scripture and Tradition outline five major steps to take that clearly and consistently challenge people on the discipleship path. Any time we ask our parishioners to do anything, the challenges are, in some way, a reflection of these steps. In each, there is a synergy between how followers grow and how the church grows.

We have come to rely on an acronym to illustrate the discipleship path: **S.T.E.P.S.** *As you read these, consider them as potential instruments to challenge the people in your pews. Mark which, if any, of these steps have been instrumental in growing your own faith.*

S: Serve in a Ministry or Mission

Service is absolutely essential to growth as a follower of Jesus Christ. Jesus said about himself that he did not come to *be* served but to serve and give his life as a ransom. Growing in discipleship requires us to have a servant's heart. As a church, if we are to make an impact on our community and world, we need people who are committed to giving their time in service.

We challenge the people in our pews to serve in ministry, which means serving at the parish and/or serving in missions, which means impacting people outside the Church. Admittedly, ministry and mission are interchangeable terms, but we use them distinctly to underscore two different types of service.

T: Tithe or Give

The Church needs financial resources to function. Ministry costs money. As people become better givers, the Church can accomplish more. But that's not why this is a step on the path toward spiritual development. God wants our hearts. Jesus constantly taught that our money and possessions often hold our hearts instead. Members of our parish need to be challenged to move from trusting their money to trusting God. The only way to go in that direction is by giving as God calls us to give: tithing, or giving away 10 percent of our income.

Tithing challenges parishioners to look at all of their finances as belonging to God and to trust him. It's a step because people need to give in their place of worship as an act of worship. We challenge the people in our pews to become *planned, priority,* and *percentage* givers as a way of moving in the direction of tithing.

E: Engage in a Small Group

St. Paul wrote, "You and I may be mutually encouraged by one another's faith, yours and mine" (Rom 1:12). We need friends in faith to grow closer to Jesus Christ. Small groups are where we provide pastoral care for our members and where our great big church gets small.

We challenge people *in* our pews to get up *out* of the pews (where they sit in rows) and get into a small group (where they sit in a circle). There, they can share their faith, learn from others' life experiences, receive support from other members, and help carry other people's burdens. We call our small groups schools for discipleship.

P: Practice Prayer; Celebrate the Sacraments

Prayer and the celebration of the sacraments help us grow in our love for God. Without them our souls can go malnourished.

We challenge members of the parish to bring all their cares and concerns before the Lord in a daily quiet time. We invite them to choose a time and place for personal prayer, helping them develop healthy habits such as scripture reading, eucharistic adoration, and the Rosary. Providing easy access to all the sacraments we especially want to help parishioners to a full and active participation in the Eucharist.

S: Share Your Faith through Evangelization

Jesus told the apostles to go and make disciples. He sent them out into the world to lead people who are unconnected to God into a relationship with him. When we share our faith and invite members into a relationship with Christ, we're helping the Church grow and we're growing too. Faith grows when it is shared.

We challenge the parishioners to share their faith through a strategy called "invest and invite." Invest in relationships in the community, and when it is right, invite them to come to church.

Reflect and Resolve

1. Take a look at your current bulletin. Based on the ads, promotions, and sales, as well as the announcements and actual parish news, what are you communicating to people about what you want them to do? If the sum total of discipleship in your parish boils down to "support the bake sale after Mass," you've got a problem.

2. Are there other steps not listed in this section that you believe are crucial to growing in faith and should be made a priority in the parish?

3. What spiritual practices are currently healthy in your parish? Which ones do you already do well?

4. What steps are lacking or are weak in your parish?

5. Which ones most excite you? Which ones are you willing to champion?

6. Reach a consensus about the steps your team will promote. Articulate the proper language to the steps that reflects your parish's culture. Write up a plan to introduce it.

Rally Cry

As a team, agree to take up the following rally cry:

> We are going to stop pandering to consumerist demands of churchpeople.

This means,

> We will start challenging them, along with ourselves, to grow as disciples.

Commit your rally cry to daily prayer. Ask God to stir in you a "holy discontent" about your rally cry; ask him to put it on your heart and help you serve it.

9
EXPECT CONFLICT

When Jesus finished all these words, he said to his disciples, "You know that in two days' time it will be Passover, and the Son of Man will be handed over to be crucified." Then the chief priests and the elders of the people assembled in the palace of the high priest, who was called Caiaphas, and they consulted together to arrest Jesus by treachery and put him to death.

MATTHEW 26:1–4

It's easy and interesting to go to conferences, read "how-to" books, or just sit around talking about what you want to do. It is a whole different deal to do something. Little did we know the season of conflict we were marching into.

REBUILT, 51

PREPARE BY READING
Rebuilt: chapter 4

Consider

The backdrop of just about every story in the scriptures is conflict or some kind of battle. The Old Testament brings interpersonal conflicts between Jacob and Esau, Moses and the Pharaoh, and David and Absalom. There are military battles as the Israelites fight to take possession of the Promised Land and, later, hold on to it, not to mention the ceaseless war the rebellious Israelites wage against God's will.

The theme of conflict continues in the gospels. Jesus battles with demons and even the devil himself. He experiences resistance from his own hometown crowd. But his most consistent conflict comes with the Pharisees and other religious leaders. That battle was basically over the meaning and purpose of the law and what it reveals about the heart of God. It was about the balance of truth and grace and the reach of the Father's mercy and love. This conflict happens over and over and over again—the story is found in all four gospels. Later, Peter, Paul, and all the apostles continue to experience persecution from religious and civil authorities as they advance the mission of the Gospel. Battle and conflict fill the story of the Bible and the history of the Church, so why are we surprised when we experience it ourselves in our parish? We can't wish it away, and we can only avoid it in the short term through inaction.

Certain kinds of conflict can be validating. If we experience conflict for the same reasons the Lord did (service to truth and grace), then we know we are on the right track. Conflict should be seen as validating if it comes after you challenge the people in the pews to take ownership of their faith and responsibility for the mission of the Church.

Not only is all of this inevitable and validating, we believe it is necessary for maturing as leaders. In order to build muscle, you must stress it and burn it out. When you encounter opposition in your parish, God is using that to grow your resolve and dedication to the mission of the Church. If approached confidently and prayerfully, it will help your team to grow. While the strife and resulting pain may seem difficult at the time, it is perfecting us to be leaders who can more successfully carry out the mission of the Gospel. God allows the conflict to help us grow our spiritual leadership muscles.

In this step, we will talk about conflict and how to deal with it.

Pray

Pray together. Begin in silent prayer, then add spontaneous prayers of thanksgiving and petition. Begin with intercessory prayer for strength in the face of criticism. Pray for your critics *and* your enemies. Then pray:

> Heavenly Father,
> your Son came to seek and save the lost
> and to challenge churchpeople
> who had become self-righteous religious consumers.

As a result of his mission, he suffered attacks and experienced conflict
at the hands of the very people who thought they were representing you.
In every situation, he acted with both courage and love.
As we examine conflict in our church, give us the grace to be like your Son.
We pray this through Christ, our Lord.
Amen.

Tell Your Story

Conflict is inevitable because we are in the midst of a spiritual battle. Changing our Church culture and growing healthy parishes is a spiritual exercise that will involve nothing less than warfare.

What is your immediate response to hearing that changing your church culture is a spiritual battle? Does it scare you? Does it fire you up? What is your reaction?

How do you naturally deal with conflict? Do you tend to respond with fight, flight, or just ignore it and hope it goes away?

Are you surprised that churchpeople are opposing efforts to make changes to the Church culture?

On a scale of one to five, what is your level of tolerance for conflict?

Read Aloud

The following is excerpted and modified from Rebuilt, *pages 58–63. We suggest breaking the reading into parts and having more than one reader.*

The conflict came not when things were *said* but when things were *done*. What we did was make church all about who *wasn't* there and started challenging who *was* there to grow. And what we did brought conflict. Every time we moved forward with this agenda, we could absolutely go to the bank that there would be criticism and attack.

Here are some of the tactics our dissatisfied, demanding consumers used in their war against us:

- *Indirect assault*: This was gossip and slander often accompanied by passive-aggressive resistance. It was more widespread and insidious than we realized at the time.
- *Direct assault*: Usually delivered immediately following Mass, this was the most honest form of complaint, but it was emotionally driven, so it was rarely clear or helpful.
- *E-mail*: Closely related to the direct assault, because it's also based in emotion, this attack was often *more* emotionally charged and therefore even *less* helpful.
- *Letter*: It is one of our axioms that cards are good, letters are bad. If someone goes to the trouble of writing a letter, nine times out of ten it will be a complaint. Complaint letters are

invariably written according to the same template: The writers present their credentials ("I've been in this parish for forty years!"). The writers present their issue. The writers present every other issue they can think of to attach to their issue, as if there was some sort of pattern they are now exposing. The writers present their final assertion that "everybody else" feels exactly the same way. It's just that they alone are courageous enough to speak up. Thus they elevate their complaint to an act of selfless courage. Oftentimes we received anonymous letters, which is the same style of letter with the gloves off.

- *Letter-writing campaign*: Here, someone organizes others into writing about their issue, so that it really does appear that "everyone else" feels the same way.
- *Threat*: Usually this form of attack was the threat of withholding money or withdrawing membership from the parish.
- *Threat of legal action*: On two occasions, unhappy consumers brought the threat of legal action into the exchange. In both cases they relied on attorneys who happened to be relatives, so they were just using cheap scare tactics . . . but they were scary.
- *Complaint to the diocese*: Any of the above could also be accompanied by a complaint to the diocese, but oftentimes veteran combatants just circumvented us and went right to the top. This approach had several advantages. It put us in our place, guaranteed a response from a high level, inflicted obvious discomfort on us, and raised their complaint to a church-wide issue.

Stop and Discuss: Do the descriptions of complaint from *Rebuilt* describe what has happened in your parish? What forms of complaint have you received? Is there any complaint or conflict you have found especially challenging?

So what were they complaining about? They were complaining about challenge and change: changes in the Mass times; changes in the weekend schedule; changes in the music; changes in the sanctuary lighting; changes to the focus and content of the weekend message; changes in anything that impacted them or forced them to alter their habits; changes that had nothing to do with them and were none of their business; and changes in approach and style for which they didn't have a context or referent. The changes in church life were unwelcome and even perceived as threats to many parishioners. But beyond any of these particular changes was the biggest change of all, the change in culture we were making: challenging churchpeople and seeking the unchurched. More than any other change, this was the one that provoked many of our churchpeople.

Of course the complaints got packaged differently. We were accused of negligence, incompetence, and malice. Supposed violations of canon law, lack of reverence for the sacraments, and disregard for liturgical rules and rubrics were often cited. And character issues were raised. Most complainers probably didn't really care about any of those things (even if they had been true). Their core complaint was always the same complaint. They were demanding consumers whose expectations were no longer being met.

We certainly didn't anticipate the difficulties we encountered, and we continued to be surprised as they kept on coming over the course of several years. One of our teammates, Sean, came to refer to our office as the "bunker." To be honest, there was some criticism that was heartfelt and sincere and even helpful. There was criticism we richly deserved, even if we didn't see it that way at the time. Through this process, there were many ways we genuinely messed up, and people had every right to complain. But most of the time it was just hurtful, and some of it was even hateful. We were wounded by the malicious nature of the attacks, the name-calling, the gossip, and the stunning slander.

Stop and Discuss: How can you learn from your critics without allowing them to throw you off course? How can you guard against critics who attempt to distract the parish?

Pastorally gifted leaders would have assisted people thoughtfully through the process and made it less painful for them. Emotionally intelligent leaders would have taken it all less personally. Spiritually mature leaders would have seen the conflict coming because Jesus told his followers to expect it. We were lacking on all these counts, but we kept moving forward.

The problem is that the status quo gets confused with the will of God. Challenging or changing anything in churchworld is equated with challenging or changing God! The attacks we experienced were sometimes so vicious because people thought they were defending their faith—when, in fact, they were defending the culture of their religion.

Reflect and Resolve

1. What lessons have you learned about how to deal with conflict and complaint well?

2. How can you respond to criticism in effective and charitable ways?

3. When it comes to conflict in the parish, there are a few ways you can get it wrong. One way is to not expect it or to naively think that if there is a problem, it must be your fault. Another potential problem is trying to avoid tough choices and difficult decisions for fear of conflict. But if you do, nothing will change. A third way to get it wrong with conflict is to take it very personally and allow it to distract you, or worse, hurt your heart. Is any of this happening?

4. Which of these temptations are you most likely to fall into moving forward? As a team, decide what action steps you are going to take with criticism, conflict, and complaint and how you will support each other during those times. (Recognize and discuss the fact that most of the criticism will be directed at the pastor or pastoral leader so special consideration should be given to how he or she will be supported.)

Rally Cry

As a team, agree to take up the following rally cry:

> We will expect conflict as we work at rebuilding our parish culture and support each other when it comes.

This means,

> We will carefully consider the validity of criticism and learn from it when we can. We will not allow criticism to settle in our hearts and not treat our detractors as the enemy. We will pray for them and ask that they pray for us. We will try to remember that in the work we do we have a real enemy, and he cannot win.

Commit your rally cry to daily prayer. Ask God to stir in you a "holy discontent" about your rally cry; ask him to put it on your heart and help you serve it.

10
LEAD WHERE YOU SERVE

The Lord brought David victory in all his undertakings. David was king over all Israel; he dispensed justice and right to all his people.

1 Chronicles 18:13–14

What is leadership? As authors and management experts Ken Blanchard and Phil Hodges point out, it's basically a process of influence. Any time you're trying to influence the thoughts and actions of others toward a new place or different outcomes, in either their personal or professional life, you're engaging in leadership. History is shaped by leaders. Nothing great ever gets accomplished without great leadership.

Rebuilt, 242

PREPARE BY READING
Rebuilt: chapter 14

Consider

Here's the simple way to know if you are a leader: take a look over your shoulder and check to see if anyone is following you.

Leadership matters. Everything rises or falls on leadership.

We see it over and over again in every endeavor: business, government, nonprofits, families, and even the Church. When leaders use their authority and influence for the good of an organization, fully engage all their skills to serve those around them, and care enough to move forward despite a fear of failure or criticism, everyone in that organization wins.

Leadership matters because every community is different. While anyone can learn from another successful organization, leadership is required to recognize transferrable principles and discern exactly what will work in a particular culture or community. Leadership matters because it takes leaders to humbly, prayerfully discern the will of God and then serve it.

Authentic, Christ-centered leadership is not just about one all-powerful leader, such as the pastor. Instead, our parishes need layers of leadership, at every level of parish life.

Over the last few years, we have had an opportunity to travel across the country and around the world speaking at conferences and diocesan gatherings. Pastors will approach us to say thanks for what we are doing and then ask, "How do I get my people on board?" In turn, sometimes at the same events, parishioners will ask, "What you say is great, but how do we get our pastor on board?" Behind the question is often the idea that if only someone else would lead we could move forward. In fact, everyone needs to exercise leadership at the level in which they serve. In this step, we will look at some of the characteristics of leadership that are vital to your parish.

Pray

Pray together. Begin in silent prayer and then add spontaneous prayers of thanksgiving and petition. Pray for your bishop and pastor; pray for parish leaders, past, present, and potential. Then pray:

> Heavenly Father,
> you lead your Church in every generation.
> You have called us to join you, to reach the lost, raise up disciples,
> and advance the kingdom of God in our generation.
> Give us courage, wisdom, and humble hearts to lead with all diligence.
> Help us to use the influence and authority you have placed in our hands
> to lead our parish.
> We pray through Christ, our Lord.
> Amen.

Tell Your Story

Who is a leader you admire from history or from afar? What makes you admire him or her? Who is a leader you have seen up close? What made you admire him or her? What does it mean to be a good leader? Do you think of yourself as a leader?

Read Aloud

The following is excerpted and modified from Rebuilt, *pages 243–252. We suggest breaking the reading into parts and having more than one reader.*

1. Be a Servant Leader

Jesus isn't just a spiritual leader. Jesus is the model for all leadership. And he leads from the Cross. If we want to be great before God, we have to be like Jesus and put other people's interests ahead of our own. It's not just service; it's becoming a servant. It's a role, not simply an activity. That's the path to great leadership. That's servanthood.

In *Good to Great,* author Jim Collins sets out to show why some companies greatly improved their performance while others, in similar circumstances, did not. He found that one essential element of a good to great company was what he called a "level 5 leader." Such leaders all demonstrate the same qualities: They blend extreme personal humility with intense professional will. They're ambitious, but their ambition is directed toward their company, not themselves. They attribute successes to others and take responsibility for failures themselves.

2. Be a Wise Leader

At the same time, seek out wise counselors. Whatever kind of parish you have, there are very successful people in your pews who can teach you lots of leadership lessons. There are parishioners you know who have good judgment that they can bring to many of the decisions you have to make. A wise leader will seek those people out, invite them to get involved, make sure they have a voice, and listen to them. Some people are wise, and some people are not, but nobody has all the wisdom they need. That's why wise leaders are people who surround themselves with wisdom.

As our parish has grown, the number of people we have involved in leadership roles has grown. It's not about meetings and committees for their own sake; rather, it's about gathering the wisdom that is around us. Currently, we have teams of advisors for finances, maintenance, technology, development, human resources, and strategic planning.

We don't have any elections—notice how they don't really do elections or take votes in the Bible. Instead, we're very careful about selecting the advisors we assemble. We don't necessarily want the most *popular* people; we seek the most *talented* people. And, in turn, we take their advice very seriously. We have also developed accountability teams who speak wisdom into our own lives. Once a month we open up about what is going on professionally and personally, and they hold us accountable for the goals we set for ourselves and the changes we need to make.

Stop and Discuss: How are you tapping into the wisdom of your community? What can you do better to surround yourselves with wise leaders?

3. Be a Leader Who Learns

We have to cultivate humility and enthusiasm to learn from others who are successfully doing what we're trying to do and avail ourselves of the resources that are available. The term "learning organization" was coined by Peter Senge and seems basic to the way successful organizations will be operating in the future in our world of ceaseless, accelerated change. The principles are simple to state but challenging to keep in focus: the interconnectedness of team members; an environment of coaching and learning; permission to fail in order to learn; and, most of all, good communication.

Currently, we build in learning time to our weekly meeting schedule and encourage staff to take work time for study time and personal development, even if that means not doing other things. We also budget what money we can to expose staff and ministry leaders to some of the energizing and inspiring conferences many of the most successful evangelical churches offer. Just getting our people into vibrant church settings, where they can see and learn from successful church leaders, is motivating. Always viewed through the lens of our Catholic faith, these experiences can sometimes even be transformational (as it was for us at Saddleback).

There are lots of ways to learn, but the place to start is always humbly before God, grounded in his word, attentive to his instruction. "Fear of the Lord is the beginning of knowledge; fools despise wisdom and discipline" (Prv 1:7).

Stop and Discuss: What can you do to make the parish more of a learning organization so that all leaders are growing?

4. Be a Leader of Courage

Actually leading anybody anywhere requires a certain amount of courage. And being the lead agent in changing a church culture these days will require a lot of it. Fortunately, that's the way we're made. Gary Haugen, founder of International Justice Mission, writes, "When it comes to being brave, we should picture the courage of Jesus—the power to fearlessly speak the truth, the freedom to selflessly love, the strength to unflinchingly stretch oneself on the cross. And the truth is, in our deepest core we were actually made to be like *that*."

Courage in parish leadership means, first of all, preaching the whole message of the Gospel, not just the parts people like to hear. It also means speaking the hard truths in a loving way; confronting the facts, even when they're brutal; making the tough calls—the ones nobody else wants to face, let alone make; and really loving the people in the *parish*, even when they're not in our *church* and sometimes when they're not lovable.

Stop and Discuss: Are there any decisions or tough choices you are delaying or not making simply because of fear?

5. Be a Leader of Faithfulness

You will not change the culture of your parish overnight or all at once. It happens slowly, so give it the time it takes and needs. You've got to keep going and not give up. Even when things are not going well and people are beginning to question you, you can't quit. You cannot abdicate your leadership role just because you're frustrated when people don't follow you.

Be a leader who perseveres. And let your faithfulness be founded in and fueled by faith. Be faithful in the Lord Jesus. Trust in his leadership and the work he has given you. As Paul instructed the leaders of the Church at Ephesus before he bid them farewell, "If only I may finish my course and the ministry that I received from the Lord Jesus, to bear witness to the gospel of God's grace" (Acts 20:24). Aim to finish the race you have set out on, to complete the work God has given you and the share you have in testifying to the Gospel.

Reflect and Resolve

1. Of the leadership qualities listed from *Rebuilt*, which one do you think is the most important? Where does the team need to grow the most?

2. Who currently holds leadership-level positions in your parish? Where is leadership being exercised in a healthy and successful way? Where, in the life of your parish, are there leadership voids or vacuums?

3. Paul says in Acts 20:24, "Yet I consider life of no importance to me, if only I may finish my course and the ministry that I received from the Lord Jesus, to bear witness to the gospel of God's grace." What does that say about Paul?

4. Why is that type of commitment so important?

Rally Cry

As a team, agree to take up the following rally cry:

> We are committed to serving our parish for the long haul.

This means,

> We will continually turn our efforts over to God, trusting in his guidance.
> We will not give up.

Commit your rally cry to daily prayer. Ask God to stir in you a "holy discontent" about your rally cry; ask him to put it on your heart and help you serve it.

CONCLUSION: YOU CAN DO THIS!

The book of Nehemiah is a story of rebuilding. The backstory is the destruction of Jerusalem at the time of the Babylonian conquest and exile. Decades later, even though many Jews had returned to the city, it remained in disrepair. The city's gates and walls, essential to its integrity and security, were utterly ruined. The vision for rebuilding comes from a Jewish exile, Nehemiah, a servant in the court of the king of Persia. Moved by news of the neglected city, he determines to rebuild it. The rest of the book tells a compelling story of how Nehemiah undertook the construction despite seemingly impossible obstacles.

Nehemiah pursued his vision, even though it meant risking the king's displeasure by simply suggesting the project and then leaving his comfortable position to undertake work that would require sacrifice. He overcame outspoken critics, plots on his life, and even internal disputes and divisions.

The book of Nehemiah is a fascinating and compelling story for anyone working to change a culture and make an impact on a community. Fascinating and compelling that is, except for chapter 3. There, in chapter 3, Nehemiah lists the construction workers, detailing precisely where they labored to rebuild the wall. The chapter goes to great lengths to describe exactly where each family laid down bricks. Perhaps, if your family members were part of that effort, it made for interesting reading. But for those of us living 2,500 years after the events, it can seem pretty tedious. So why is it in the Bible?

Perhaps it is a reminder that what we do *matters*.

You can look at your parish and wonder if the work you are doing there is of any significance. In so many places, the Church has lost authority as it continues to hemorrhage members and finds itself increasingly irrelevant. So what can a single parish do?

During the rebuilding of the wall around Jerusalem, the families who rebuilt, brick by brick, wondered perhaps whether their small section of the wall mattered. But when they saw the completed project, they knew their individual efforts were essential to their collective success.

Our work is not unlike Nehemiah's reconstruction program: together with Christ, we're charged with rebuilding his Church in our generation. Like the people of Jerusalem, we all have our place on the "wall"; it's called our parish. We are laying bricks, one brick at a time, as we reach out to the lost and make disciples of Jesus Christ. And one day, maybe not in this life, probably on the other side of eternity, we will look back and recognize the eternal consequences of our work.

Meanwhile, we can undertake this work with renewed enthusiasm and fresh efforts. We can be honest about our problems. We can create excellent weekend experiences that honor God and inspire people. We can lead our parishioners to take ownership of their faith and get to work in ministry and mission. We can form communities that care about lost people and help them grow as disciples.

We can rebuild the Church, one changed life at a time.

REFERENCES
AND RESOURCES

Collins, Jim. *Good to Great.* New York: HarperCollins, 2001.

———. *How the Mighty Fall.* New York: HarperCollins, 2009.

Collins, Jim, and Jerry Porras. *Built to Last.* New York: HarperCollins, 2002.

Francis. *Evangelii Gaudium* (The Joy of the Gospel). Vatican City: Libraria Editrice Vaticana, 2013.

Haugen, Gary A. *Just Courage: God's Great Expedition for the Restless Christian.* Downer's Grove, IL: IVP, 2008.

Heath, Chip, and Dan Heath. *Made to Stick.* New York: Random House, 2007.

———. *Switch: How to Change Things When Change Is Hard.* New York: Broadway Books, 2010.

Hybels, Bill. *Holy Discontent: Fueling the Fire That Ignites Personal Vision.* Grand Rapids, MI: Zondervan, 2007.

John Paul II. *Christifideles Laici* (Christ's Faithful People). Vatican City: Libraria Editrice Vaticana, 1998.

———. *Dies Domini.* Vatican City: Libraria Editrice Vaticana, 1998.

Kinnaman, David, and Gabe Lyons. *Unchristian: What a New Generation Really Thinks About Christianity—and Why It Matters.* Grand Rapids, MI: Baker, 2007.

Lencioni, Patrick. *The Advantage: Why Organizational Health Trumps Everything Else in Business.* San Francisco: Jossey-Bass, 2012.

———. *The Five Dysfunctions of a Team: A Leadership Fable.* San Francisco: Jossey-Bass, 2002.

———. *Politics, Silos and Turf Wars: A Leadership Fable.* San Francisco: Jossey-Bass, 2006.

Mallon, James. *Divine Renovation.* Toronto: Novalis, 2014.

Mancini, Will. *Church Unique.* San Francisco: Jossey-Bass, 2008.

Rainer, Thom. *Breakout Churches.* Grand Rapids, MI: Zondervan, 2005.

———. *Surprising Insights from the Unchurched and Proven Ways to Reach Them.* Grand Rapids, MI: Zondervan, 2005.

Rainer, Thom, and Eric Geiger. *Simple Church.* Nashville: Broadman and Holman, 2006.

Ratzinger, Joseph. *The Spirit of the Liturgy.* San Francisco: Ignatius Press, 2000.

Second Vatican Council. *Lumen Gentium* (Dogmatic Constitution on the Church). Vatican City: Libraria Editrice Vaticana, 1964.

Senge, Peter. *The Fifth Discipline.* New York: Doubleday, 2006.

Stanley, Andy. *Deep and Wide: Creating Churches Unchurched People Love to Attend.* Grand Rapids, MI: Zondervan, 2012.

Warren, Rick. *The Purpose Driven Church.* Grand Rapids, MI: Zondervan, 1995.

Church of the Nativity Resources

Church of the Nativity in Timonium, MD. http://churchnativity.tv.
On Facebook www.facebook.com/churchnativity.
Nativity's Online Campus http://churchnativity.churchonline.org.
Matter Conference http://matterconference.tv.

Wesley, Christopher. *Marathon Youth Ministry* (blog). www.christopherwesley.org.
On Twitter @chrisrwesley.

White, Michael. *Make Church Matter* (blog). http://nativitypastor.tv.
On Twitter @nativitypastor.

Rebuilt Resources

Rebuilt Parish. http://rebuiltparish.com.

Rebuilt Parish Association. http://rebuiltparishassociation.com.

Rebuilt podcast. https://itunes.apple.com/us/podcast/rebuilt-podcast/id645574414?mt=2.

Wesley, Christopher. *Rebuilding Youth Ministry: Ten Practical Strategies for Catholic Parishes.* Notre Dame, IN: Ave Maria Press, 2015.

White, Michael, and Tom Corcoran. *Rebuilding Your Message: Practical Tools to Strengthen Your Preaching and Teaching.* Notre Dame, IN: Ave Maria Press, 2015.

———. *Rebuilt: Awakening the Faithful, Reaching the Lost, Making Church Matter.* Notre Dame, IN: Ave Maria Press, 2013.

———. *Tools for Rebuilding: 75 Really, Really Practical Ways to Make Your Parish Better.* Notre Dame, IN: Ave Maria Press, 2013.

TOM CORCORAN received his bachelor's degree from Loyola University Maryland and studied theology at Franciscan University of Steubenville. Corcoran has served Church of the Nativity in a variety of roles that give him a unique perspective on parish ministry and leadership. First hired as a youth minister, Corcoran has also served as coordinator of children's ministry and director of small groups.

Corcoran is associate to the pastor and is responsible for weekend message development, strategic planning, and staff development. He is the coauthor of *Rebuilt*—which narrates the story of Nativity's rebirth—*Tools for Rebuilding*, and *Rebuilding Your Message*. When he is not working, Corcoran enjoys spending time with his wife, Mia, and their seven children, who are homeschooled in Parkville, Maryland.

MICHAEL WHITE earned his bachelor's degree from Loyola University Maryland and his graduate degrees in sacred theology and ecclesiology from the Pontifical Gregorian University in Rome. After being ordained a priest of the Archdiocese of Baltimore, he worked for five years as personal secretary to Cardinal William Keeler, who was then archbishop. During that time, White served as the director of the papal visit of Pope John Paul II to Baltimore.

During White's tenure as pastor at Church of the Nativity, the church has almost tripled in weekend attendance. More important, commitment to the mission of the Church has grown, evidenced by the significant increase of giving and service in ministry, and much evidence of genuine spiritual renewal. White is the coauthor of *Rebuilt*—which narrates the story of Nativity's rebirth—*Tools for Rebuilding*, and *Rebuilding Your Message*.

The bestselling Rebuilt series has established White and Corcoran as sought-after speakers across the United States. They have also addressed dioceses in Austria, Australia, Canada, Ireland, and Poland. *Rebuilt* has been translated into several languages.

AVE

AVE MARIA PRESS

Founded in 1865, Ave Maria Press,
a ministry of the Congregation of
Holy Cross, is a Catholic publishing
company that serves the spiritual and
formative needs of the Church and its
schools, institutions, and ministers;
Christian individuals and families; and
others seeking spiritual nourishment.

———— ❦ ————

For a complete listing of titles from

Ave Maria Press

Sorin Books

Forest of Peace

Christian Classics

visit www.avemariapress.com

AVE MARIA PRESS
Notre Dame, IN
A Ministry of the United States Province of Holy Cross